Razed Monuments

poems by

Tim Heerdink

Finishing Line Press
Georgetown, Kentucky

Razed Monuments

Copyright © 2020 by Tim Heerdink
ISBN 978-1-64662-378-5 First Edition
All rights reserved under International and Pan-American Copyright Conventions. No part of this book may be reproduced in any manner whatsoever without written permission from the publisher, except in the case of brief quotations embodied in critical articles and reviews.

Acknowledgements

The author would like to thank Eva Mozes Kor for being a hero and role model to many. Her message of forgiveness shall live on forever. May she rest in peace knowing that her life had purpose and was fulfilled. He'd also like to thank his wife and daughter, Amber and Audrey, whose love carries him through when poetry is not enough. Gratitude also goes to all those along the way who have shown support to C.A.N.D.L.E.S. and to the love of sharing words and time.

He'd also like to thank the journals and anthologies of which some of these poems have been previously published, sometimes in earlier forms.

Poetry Quarterly, Summer 2019: "Needleman"
Flying Island Journal: "Farewell Fanfare in B Minor"
Midnight Special: "Recycling the Obsolete: 2020"
Avalanches in Poetry: "Flowers for Hitler"
Midwest Writers Guild Literary Journal, Volume 1: "Masks"

"Lady in Blue," "A-7064," "Farewell Fanfare in B Minor," and "Notre Dame en Flammes" are also published in the poetry collection, *The Human Remains* (Bird Brain Publishing, 2019).

"Not Yet, Pista" is reprinted with permission from the author, Stephen Nasser. It first appeared in his book, *Journey to Freedom* (Nasser, 2015).

Publisher: Leah Maines
Editor: Christen Kincaid
Cover Art and Design: François Vaillancourt
Author Photo: Amber Heerdink
Dedication Photo: Linda Zignego. Courtesy of Alex Kor.

Order online: www.finishinglinepress.com
also available on amazon.com

Author inquiries and mail orders:
Finishing Line Press
P. O. Box 1626
Georgetown, Kentucky 40324
U. S. A.

Contents

Foreword by John Guzlowski 1

"Not Yet, Pista" by Stephen "Pista" Nasser 2

Lady in Blue 4

A-7064 5

Field of Dreams 6

The Bell Still Rings in Hamburg 7

Razed Monuments 8

Notre Dame en Flammes 10

I am Not a Jew 11

Arbeit Macht Frei 12

Needleman 13

A Final Repose before the Gallows 14

Farewell Fanfare in B Minor 15

Recycling the Obsolete: 2020 16

Masks 17

Flowers for Hitler 18

Kanada 19

Block 11 20

Seventh of December 21

Toleration 23

Roll Call 24

At Nighttime, Wir Sprechen Deutsch 25

Hidden 26

Golden Path of the Resistant 28

Fingering the Switch 29

*This book is dedicated to Eva Mozes Kor,
our Lady in Blue
(January 31, 1934 – July 4, 2019)*

Foreword

The world is full of people who don't want to think about the reality of war and genocide.

They want to imagine that the world has turned a corner and that we've evolved away from the dark past of the Holocaust and the 50 million and more deaths of World War II. It's not hard to imagine why.

But this is why we need writers like Tim Heerdink. He has somehow learned the valuable lesson that terrible things like the Holocaust have happened in the past and they may certainly happen again.

In his book, *Razed Monuments*, Heerdink looks around and sees the world beneath the world of TV shows and sports events and celebrations of this and that. It's a world where the memory of the Holocaust still touches him, a world where politicians promise us safety and security but deliver something else, a world where the promise of peace and joy and pleasure is a fairy tale told by a killer dressed in grandma's rags.

Heerdink sees his job as a writer is to warn us that the reality we want is not the reality that is actually before us.

Like all good writers, he is a prophet you shouldn't ignore.

>   —**John Guzlowski**, author of *Echoes of Tattered Tongues: Memory Unfolded*, *True Confessions*, and *The Third Winter of War: Buchenwald*

Not Yet, Pista

First Andris, then Pista, brothers
were born onto the sea of life.
To a family of loving parents
were protected from harm and strife.

They sailed through happy childhood
educated side by side.
Andris was Pista's hero
and was never let out of his sight.

As they grew up year by year,
they created a tight bond to last
never to be broken
by any storm Evil can cast.

As clouds of despair darkened the sky,
the brothers found strength and trust
in each other's company
even the rough seas could not bust.

Growing up became a challenge
as the Nazis stormed in their life,
tossed them apart from the ones they loved,
and took their family, never to be found alive.

At a tender age, the orphans were deported
to Auschwitz Death Camp.
Beaten, starved, and degraded,
their love gave them inner strength.

Losing strength and lots of weight,
their survival was to degrade.
Pista wrote his diary
assured his hope would never fade.

Andris weakened by the day
tossed around the storm of fate.
Pista made a promise to his brother
he would never give up, and stayed in shape.

Andris passed in his brother's arms,
the Nazis succeeded in killing the brother
but failed to break their bond
and the love they had for one another.

The fury of the storm has passed,
Pista kept his promise to his brother,
he shared his diary and spread the word
as they had agreed one to the other.

The seas have never calmed.
As years gone by, memories have faded,
but Andris and Pista's bond
will never be degraded.

As unconscious Pista was liberated,
he thought he saw his brother in heaven.
He called out, "I want to be with you!"
Andris replied, "Not Yet, Pista! You have time given."

> **—Stephen "Pista" Nasser**, Holocaust survivor and
> author of *My Brother's Voice* and *Journey to Freedom*

Lady in Blue
for Eva Mozes Kor

Torn from her mother
like two poles of opposites,
childhood ended
at the selection platform.
With the mate from the womb,
a pact to survive
the frost, hunger, and slaughter
among the endless obstacles
that lied within the walls of Hell.
Staring the Angel of Death in the face
as he poked and recorded the outcome,
knowing that someday
there'd be reason
for dancing,
hands in the air
as the rest of the world cheered
in victory;
forgiveness the key.

A-7064
for Miriam Mozes Zeiger

A familiar stench drifts in the atmosphere of the parlor
where I bury my face and contemplate
the past and what comes next.
Every inch must be sterile and in its right place
before my thought train can jolt to a halt.
In 2019,
bets are in your favor
when you throw a dart in a bundle of people
the one who strikes you down in return
bares marked skin
for the sake of art or to belong if nothing else.
My bouquet has an eternal bloom upon my arm
never to wither and descend to dust
unless the rest of me follows.
About ten pieces into my transformation
and still there remains a flutter
just as the gun begins to buzz.
What went through Miriam's mind
as Eva kicked and fought her tattooist?
Knowing her number comes next,
she could bring further Mozes fury
or sit and take the inevitable.
The only choice; to survive.

Field of Dreams

Politicians looking for a lasting namesake
or a quick payday to line their pockets
explain why Roberts Stadium is nothing
but a patch of grass and a memory.
Evansville had no need for a new arena
downtown where the rest of the businesses starve.
No place to park but a stake in our hearts
as a team who made threats leaves for south
after a couple of years in their newly financed home
paid by citizens who would've preferred the building
where they had their first concert,
graduated from high school,
maybe even had a prom or two.
So many events remain in the past
for a place that had great plans
but continues to push up only grass.
If only our mayor visited the capital of Germany
to take a stroll through the open park of a closed airport.
The big metallic birds don't fly down those lanes anymore,
and yet, there's plenty of activity at Flughafen Berlin-Tempelhof.

The Bell Still Rings in Hamburg

Year of the apocalypse fabled to begin with the start of winter,
a speed train brought me to a wonderful place
im Herzen von Deutschland.[1]
I reenact a beheading of a pirate, my brother,
for all the onlookers
who want to be entertained.
Hasn't this land seen enough bloodshed?
Let the symphony hall be built to great heights
and tell us stories of romance and adventure.
I want to hear those cellos sing.
Come on, woodwinds,
we all know you're back there,
hiding where only those from the sky can see.
Sooth me with a tune when my eyes are closed,
for when I wake,
there is a chapel in ruins from firefights
and continuous bombing toward the end of the war.
Standing as a memorial to prevent passersby
from letting history slip back to bad mistakes.
Despite being charred and abandoned
as a place of worship,
when invisible forces you can only see *vom Himmel*[2]
exhale a slight sigh in remembrance,
alone in the opened dark tower
a bell still rings.

---

1 German for "in the heart of Germany."
2 German for "from Heaven."

Razed Monuments

Grand structures erected by the broken backs
forced to labor because option number two
called for a mixture of torture before ending
life, the one thing we all hold on to
when possessions descend to ash,
also have a limited existence.

Some so ambitious,
drawers of the blueprints
fail to see their mind's
architecture executed.
Generations pass along
the task to create great wonder.

Allied bombs strip culture,
and the past weeps
as bricks and bodies
collide with the earth.

Deniers seize any
opportunity available
to discredit what is truth.
Barracks and crematoria
blasted to cover evidence
once the war took a turn.
To preserve memory,
replicas stand in place
while some are left
in ruins.

Testimony from millions
cannot be chalked up
as false propaganda.
Where did the survivors
gather for collaboration
so the recalling of events
could match
like lost pieces
in a broken puzzle?

Buildings aren't just walls
but the stories of all who've passed
the thresholds along the way.

Notre Dame en Flammes

Pourquoi, pourquoi![3]
    J'aime tes belle tours
pointant vers le ciel
    avec grâce et facilité.
Que les feux ne tuent pas
    la mémoire.
C'est vraiment dommage.

Our Lady in Flames

Why, why!
    I love your beautiful towers
pointing to the sky
    with grace and ease.
May the fire not kill
    the memory.
It's a shame.

---

3 French poem written the day the Notre Dame cathedral in Paris, France burned.

I am Not a Jew

I am not a Jew
               but a Hoosier Protestant
     turned agnostic
         due to my state of confusion
as of late.

I am not a Jew,
        my response when asked
     why I care so much
             when it comes to the Holocaust.
My rebuttal,
        How can one care
                so little?
Jews weren't the only ones
        targeted for their identity.
   Homosexuals, Gypsies, the disabled,
     Soviets, and political opponents also fell
at the command of Hitler.
I am not a Jew
     nor am I with the Nazis.
Coming from Dutch descent,
              I am the fruit of men who left
     to cross the Atlantic
back in the 1850s.
     Even with the hint of German
   mixed in with the rest,
I can only feel guilt
        if I choose to let the memory
     of millions who have perished
        flicker out and pass with closed lips.
No, I am not a Jew,
        but I stand for anyone
who needs a voice
        and a hand.
               The Holocaust shall never be forgotten.
  We must always remember
            what we've done
and stop the forces that be
     before it happens again.

Arbeit Macht Frei

     ARBEIT   MACHT   FREI

The	lie
evil	men
told	those

transported from faraway lands to an unspeakable torment meant to dehumanize so the ultimate plan of ridding the undesired can be out of the sight and minds of the everyday citizens living free.

Almost	eighty
years	after,
and	now

there are photographs of foolish individuals jumping with joy in a place where many were separated from their families as confusion put mental restraints after the journey.

Deniers	desire
history	to be
forgotten,	rewritten
for an agenda	implemented
on the new	generations.
Such	disrespect
shall	not
be	taken
very	lightly.
Never	forget,
always	remember
the	Holocaust.

Needleman

    Positioned in the intersection where two walls collide
lies a figure with a top hat ten inches tall
     and a grin which never seems to be at ease.
A silence engulfs the space between you and the void
begging for the epiphany to blossom like a perennial
      seventy-nine days since the last warm sunshine.
   Adjacent a vintage stereo sits a rack of records,
some dating back to the days before the bombs fell
      to put an end to the last world war.
What will it be today, sir?
 Shall I put on the Wagner
      or something a bit more modern?
   asks the apparition anticipating an answer
    powerful enough to transfer all present to another place,
another time, where all the outside disappears.
   Placing the needle elates the towering fellow
     like his sole purpose is fulfilled that very moment
  and he is free to be absorbed back into the drywall
after a tip of his brim,
      knowing music fills the halls once more.

A Final Repose before the Gallows

Block the light out from your eyes on this thundering night
with its menacing cracks that flash like insults
meant to pierce armor and belittle the sensitive hidden
on the inside.
Take all the oxygen possible
while these moments allow such action.
Men are preparing your knot just around the corner,
painstakingly double-checking the adequacy to ensure
the neck which holds your crime-thinking head
snaps.
Travel back to a time where the chance to share your voice,
protest, act, vote, stand up saw no consequence
for you were free.
A window of opportunity shattered by idle hands
who figured nothing could get worse
until it did.

Now we're all in cages,
waiting for our number to be called
so this dance of all dances can finally end.

Farewell Fanfare in B Minor

All the horns blow simultaneously in tune
for the ones being marched to a still moment.
Let the singers serenade with their swan songs
while the majority pray that wood can triumph over flame.
The Sun shall rise on the very last day,
waving its rays to welcome Earth and its terminal inhabitants.
Hell, the birds may decide to whistle as well in rejoice.

I've heard one network has an orchestral broadcast
set to play *Nearer, My God, to Thee*
when the sky begins to fall.
It's also been said that a band used the same hymn
to calm the doomed
who couldn't escape the Titanic.
Someone must have taken note
and thought it not their time to depart.

Surely, there'll be others running from Death
or glued to the silver screens as often is the case,
watching overpaid suits quickly lose their thought process
as pools of perspiration mixed with tears blind them from the present.

There's no hiding from the dark angel forever.
Instead of joining in the looting and chaos,
my plan is to embrace my girls
and let the Tchaikovsky vinyl sooth us,
knowing there's no place I'd rather be.

Recycling the Obsolete: 2020

Last month, lawmakers signed a bill stating that surgeons can refuse
operations for any citizens over the age of seventy years,
leaving the elderly to question where they fit in a society
which only cares for the young and healthy.
Not the unborn, though.
That's too young to be a matter of importance;
too small to give a moment's care.
Extract living people out of individuals
who have better things to do than be parents.

Our respect for human life is almost nonexistent.
Those who claim to never forget the Holocaust
stand by while a genocide claims its victims
like a debt never fully paid
due to the collected interest.

Blood acts as both fuel and currency,
and let's speak the clear truth:
it's not about rights but dead presidents
mixed with a great amount of power
to control the population
from repopulating
and growing old.

Masks

Uncover your face.
The devil's night has passed,
and we aren't children any longer.
Be real for once,
because truth is everything
this world needs.

Flowers for Hitler

Beautiful for a day
        until the entropy causes the petals
like dictators
        to fall.
Flowers for Hitler,
        a title for two books.
One by the legendary Mike Whicker,
        the other a long lost collection
penned by the hand of the late
        Mr. Leonard Cohen.
Controversial in its day to speak
        of a man who ended innocent lives,
    Cohen's third publication
        slipped out of print,
    leaving Ilse Dorsch's story
        the only one to be told.
A bouquet for *the nice man*
    who later ripped the petals of family
and tossed them aside
        in his destructive path across Europe.

Kanada

Whisked away in the night
at the hands of the Gestapo
without a moment's notice,
home had to be collected.
The important things must go.
Of course, the children hid their dolls,
the ladies jewelry and the wardrobe.
Men packed cigarettes
not knowing of their value
as currency
once the wives and children
disappeared.
Gold fillings from silenced mouths
aside wedding banners
used to make the wicked wealthy.
Mouths that screamed
as Zyklon B dropped
from the ceiling hatch.
Hands that once held a lover
scratching to break free.
Free from the poison
which claimed many.
A collection of possessions
into piles reminiscent of the bodies
tossed aside to be burned after
the shower and the pain ceased.

Enough combs and shoes to testify
one of humanity's darkest hours.
The hair in abundance
screams through the glass
at passersby who travel to witness
remains of what people used to hold dear
before their country turned against them.

Block 11

Within every man-made establishment
lies the pinnacle of progress and digression
tugging at each other's epidermis
in a fight to come out ahead.

The penultimate point of human suffering
Auschwitz I offered the prisoners;
a hell inside the prison
where torture and death
are the only outcome.

No windows in the cells
where unfortunate innocents
hanged for extended periods
with chains wrapped around arms
behind backs, dislocating shoulders
in darkness.

A wall on the side to set an example
for any who contemplated
stepping out of line.
Blood splattered brick
and worn out nooses
haunt the memory
of a nation that'd rather
forget.

Past is present,
and walls continue to hold secrets.
I believe there are victims
on both sides.
When does the healing begin?

Seventh of December

Many desire change for the world
but lack the motivation for action
until conflict hits home
where it hurts.
Europe had its war for years
before Japan brought America
out from its dormant state
to unite for the great cause.
The Axis of Evil already devastated
a great number of locations
which held beauty left in ruins.
A sneak attack on Pearl Harbor
one calm morning
while plenty rested from the night
filled with parties the day before
changed countless lives.
Revenge on the stranger
and anyone who looked like them
rolled down that terrific mountain
like a snowball of hate.
Internment camps to imprison neighbors,
friends to make sure no spying
or further attacks
could hit from the inside.
I look today
at the people in cages
and wonder,
*What have these people done
to deserve this?*
How are we any better
than America back then?
The people we celebrated
until another turned them against us?

We lie down with our mouths shut
not because a gun is facing our direction
but for the same reason it's been
throughout our bloody existence.
A prayer that all the bad
shall surely fix itself
and our own responsibility
is not necessary.

Toleration

I asked a young boy while on tour
as he joyfully passed my table of books
if supporting C.A.N.D.L.E.S.
with the purchase of my first collection
to spread Holocaust knowledge
gave him any interest.
Confused and a bit disturbed,
the boy turned to his father,
asking what in the world
I was talking about.
By the tween age,
images of the event
never reached this child.
It is becoming common
for reads like *Night*
and *The Diary of a Young Girl*
to be optional
or not offered at all
since many parents are claiming
their children may feel *uncomfortable*.
If we can't tolerate feeling
uncomfortable,
what will happen
when someone makes us upset?
What if they are
different?
Shall we rid of them as well?

Roll Call

Today, just like any other,
we stood for hours
while the SS checked our numbers.
Yes, numbers, for names are forgotten
when you're made to appear
as rats.

Eliezer passed on the night before last,
yet we still carry him to the line.
If anyone is missing,
we're all punished.
Runaways get hanged
or shot
while anyone holding secrets
feels the wrath
our captors lack the need for an excuse
to reign upon us.

The sun falls back to sleep
before black water
passed off as coffee,
sawdust bread,
and *Gemüse* are served.
None of it is enough
for all the malnourished stomachs
growling after the day's harshness.

As long as we can continue
showing up at roll call,
breathing the ashen air
produced from the ones we've lost,
one day
there will come a time
to testify.

At Nighttime, Wir Sprechen Deutsch

Die Sonne geht unter[4]
und wir können uns selbst sein.
Sie denken,
dass wir schuldig sind,
aber die Vergangenheit
ist nicht uns.
Unsere Zungen sehnen sich
nach der Sprache,
die sie als Kind
zum ersten Mal sangen.
Wir müssen unser Erbe
in diesen dunklen Zeiten
am Leben erhalten.
In der Nacht
können wir frei sein.

At Nighttime, We Speak German

The sun sets
and we can be ourselves.
They think,
that we are guilty,
but the past
is not us.
Our tongues long
for the language,
first used to sing
in infancy.
We must keep
our heritage alive
in these dark times.
At night,
we can be free.

---

4 German poem about hiding one's nationality with language.

Hidden

Dig deep,
        find the courage it takes
to bring the truth to light.
           Many great things are left
    hidden.
        One's own identity
should flourish
        and be celebrated
   like the uniqueness
lost worlds dream of
when feigning sleep.
So many homosexuals
        hide behind mirrored hetero
tendencies
        so they can be accepted
and embraced
        instead of being disowned,
   cast out from the family
or society in some cases.

Countless Jews sought shelter
        with word of the Gestapo
making arrests,
        placing stripped citizens
in ghettos
       and later camps
           which held a rumor
    of being synonymous
with death
        as time limped forward.

Ending a life
        for being
what cannot be changed.
          Hate spread through fear,
  propaganda's desired result.
Today is no different
    than any page in the book
  of our past.
  There's always a target,
              a scapegoat.

May it be a socially shy child,
an immigrant
      seeking asylum,
  or an individual
born in the wrong body,
      we should open up
  our doors
and adopt a new motto:
            Welcome all.

Golden Path of the Resistant

Taking a late afternoon walk
    along the *Viscardigasse*
        in Munich,
      Bavaria's loving heart,
     transfers feet and mind back
    to a time where Nazis ruled.

    You can look down,
see the stones paved with gold.
It's subtle
such as the way of resistance.

A monument for the lives lost
    from Hitler's failed attempt
      to seize the city
       during the 1923 Beer Hall Putsch
      guarded by soldiers
        who forced pedestrians to salute
          one arm diagonal
       in honor of *der Führer*.

      Those who did not obey
    found themselves inside the walls
      of Dachau.
   After enough arrests,
a new path to detour the threat
allowed citizens against the regime
    safe passage to work.

      Breaking the law
        does not speak of ethics.
    As I reach the end of the street
    and return to the present,
  I can't help but feel
a change in my direction.

Fingering the Switch

I want to turn you
on.
Turn you to read,
to think critically.
Bring your mind to poetry
and into conversations
many tend to steer clear.
Let me slide
my fingers deep
inside that starving brain
you keep locked
in a mental cell.

I can feel the switch.
Yes,
that's the spot
right there.
Literature used to hold
favor amongst many.
Where did we go wrong?
Don't shut yourself
away.

This isn't about money
but the fall of ideas.
Can I plant the seed
of hope and peace
for you to bloom and let shine
years after my bones turn
back to dust?

Too often invitations go
rejected
like my intellectual courting
sputters without drive.
I no longer pray,
but if there must be a last request,
may it be
that my poetic language
does not go over
your head.

Tim Heerdink is the author of three poetry collections, *The Human Remains, Red Flag and Other Poems, Razed Monuments*, and the novel, *Last Lights of a Dying Sun*. Heerdink is president of the Midwest Writers Guild. His short stories, *The Tithing of Man* and *HEA-VEN2*, won first and second place in the guild's annual anthology contests. He also has poems published in *Poetry Quarterly, Fish Hook, Flying Island, Kissing Dynamite, Auroras & Blossoms, Tanka Journal, Landslide Lit, As It Ought To Be Magazine, Rogue Wolf, Alien Buddha, Madness Muse Press*, and various anthologies. He graduated from USI with a BA in English and resides in Newburgh, Indiana with his wife, daughter, dog, and two cats.

www.ingramcontent.com/pod-product-compliance
Lightning Source LLC
LaVergne TN
LVHW041508070426
835507LV00012B/1403